Table of Contents

Unit 1 School Days — page 2
Unit 2 Weekend Fun — page 10

Units 1–2 Listen and Review — page 18
Let's Read About the Secret Message — page 19

Unit 3 Going Shopping — page 20
Unit 4 Around Town — page 28

Units 3–4 Listen and Review — page 36
Let's Read About the Text Message — page 37

Unit 5 Explore the World — page 38
Unit 6 Doing Things — page 46

Units 5–6 Listen and Review — page 54
Let's Read About the Hidden Gold — page 55

Unit 7 About Me — page 56
Unit 8 In the Future — page 64

Units 7–8 Listen and Review — page 72
Let's Read About the Surprise Party — page 73

Syllabus — page 74
Teacher and Student Card List — page 76
Word List — page 77

Hi, I'm Ginger!

Hi, I'm Sam!

Let's Start

Let's Build

Let's Learn

Units Review

Let's Read

Let's Read About

Unit 1 School Days

Let's Start

A. Let's talk.

Kate: Whose mittens are those?
Jenny: They're Anna's mittens.
Kate: Which girl is Anna?
Jenny: She's the girl who is watering the plants.

Kate: Whose scarf is that?
Jenny: It's Anna's scarf.
Kate: What about that hat?
Jenny: That's hers, too.

Kate: Is that her glove, too?
Jenny: No, it isn't. I think it's Jim's glove.
Kate: Which boy is Jim?
Jenny: He's the boy who is looking for his other glove.

B. Let's practice.

Whose hat is that?
It's Anna's hat.
It's hers.

It's my hat. = It's mine.
It's your hat. = It's yours.
It's his hat. = It's his.

It's her hat. = It's hers.
They're our hats. = They're ours.
They're their hats. = They're theirs.

C. Practice the words and sentences.

1. watering the plants
2. feeding the fish
3. writing on the board
4. talking to the teacher
5. reading a textbook
6. writing an essay
7. doing some homework
8. looking for something

> Anna is the girl who is watering the plants.

D. Ask and answer. Ask questions about the picture above.

> Which girl is Anna?   She's the girl who is watering the plants.

Let's Learn

 What was he doing when the bell rang?
He was talking on his cell phone.

A. Practice the words. 〔CD 1 07〕

1. talking on his cell phone

2. listening to music

3. taking a nap

4. reading a magazine

5. cleaning his room

6. writing a message

B. Practice the sentences.

> He was talking on his cell phone when the bell rang.
> When the bell rang, he was talking on his cell phone.

4 Unit 1 / School Days

C. Practice the question and answer.

| What was he doing when the bell rang? | He was talking on his cell phone. |

1.
2.
3.
4.
5.
6.

D. Ask and answer. Ask questions about the pictures above.

| Was he talking on his cell phone when the bell rang? | Yes, he was.
 No, he wasn't. |

Unit 1 / School Days 5

Let's Read

A. Read the new words.

| ice pops | invent → invented | outside |
| mix → mixed | stick | frozen |

B. Read.

THE FIRST ICE POP

Do you like ice pops? Today kids all around the world enjoy ice pops. Did you know that an eleven-year-old boy invented them in 1905?

One cold winter night, Frank was making soda water outside. He added soda powder to water and mixed it with a   . He was mixing his drink when his mother called. "Come inside, Frank," she said. "It's time for bed."

Frank forgot to take his drink with him. In the morning, the soda water was frozen. He pulled the stick out of the cup and looked at the first ice pop.

C. Choose another title.

   a. How to Make an Ice Pop
   b. The History of Ice Pops
   c. Frank's Frozen Soda Water

D. Answer the questions.

1. Who invented the ice pop?
2. How did Frank make soda water?
3. Why did Frank leave the water outside?
4. What happened to the water?
5. Did Frank want to make an ice pop?

E. Understand the vocabulary.

> An eleven-year-old boy invented them in 1905.

What does the word invent mean?
   a. make something
   b. make something for the first time
   c. make something many times

F. Understand the grammar.

> He was mixing his drink when his mother called.

Which sentence has about the same meaning?
   a. First Frank was mixing his drink. Then his mother called.
   b. First Frank's mother called. Then he mixed his drink.

G. Your turn.

Think of two questions about the reading. Ask your partner.

H. What about you?

Do you like ice pops? What's your favorite flavor?

Let's Build

A. Practice the grammar chant. 🎵 CD1 15

Whose boots are these?
Whose boots are these?
Whose boots are these?
  They're mine. They're my boots.

Whose hat is that? Whose hat is that?
Whose hat is that?
  It's his. It's his hat.

Whose socks are those?
Whose socks are those?
Whose socks are those?
  They're hers. They're her socks.

This coat is his. That coat is hers.
These gloves are mine. They're mine!

B. Ask and answer. 🎵 CD1 16

> Whose scarf is it?   Whose jeans are they?
>   It's Anna's scarf. It's hers.   They're Jeff's jeans. They're his.

Emily   Zack   Jeff   Anna   Megan   Tony

8 Unit 1 / School Days

C. Make sentences.

watch TV
listen to music
wash his / her face
read a book
do homework
eat spaghetti

Bill was reading a book when the doorbell rang.

D. Ask and answer. Ask questions about the picture above.

Which boy is Bill?   He's the boy who is reading a book.

Unit 2 Weekend Fun

 Let's Start

A. Let's talk. CD1 20

Scott: You went to the circus last weekend, didn't you?
Jenny: Yes, I did. It was wonderful!
Scott: Did you see the clowns?
Jenny: Yes, I did. I saw the acrobats and jugglers, too. They were amazing.

Scott: What did the jugglers do?
Jenny: They juggled balls, fruit, and chairs. Some of the jugglers were clowns, too.
Scott: Were the clowns funny?
Jenny: Yes, they were. It was a great show.

Scott: What about the acrobats?
Jenny: I went backstage before the show and saw them practice. I was amazed.
Scott: Why?
Jenny: Because they're so strong. I stood on an acrobat's shoulders. It was exciting!

B. Let's practice. CD1 21

You went to the circus last weekend, didn't you?	Yes, I did.
	No, I didn't.

C. Say these.

1. The acrobats were amazing.
   She was amazed.

2. Backstage was interesting.
   He was interested.

3. The clowns were frightening.
   He was frightened.

4. The juggler was disappointing.
   She was disappointed.

D. Practice the sentences.

> The juggler was amazing.   She was amazed.

1. acrobat / disappointing

2. tiger / frightening

3. juggler / amazing

4. backstage / interesting

Let's Learn

What did he say?
He said the ice cream was delicious.

A. Say these.

1.  The acrobat is beautiful.
2. The man is strong.
3.  The dancers are graceful.
4.  The clowns are silly.
5.  The T-shirt is expensive.
6.  The ice cream is delicious.

B. Make sentences.

The acrobat is beautiful.   He said the acrobat was beautiful.

say → said
is → was
are → were

The acrobat is beautiful.
He said the acrobat was beautiful.

Unit 2 / Weekend Fun

C. Practice the question and answer.

What did he say?	He said it was delicious.
He	said	he	was sad.
She		she	
They	said	they	were amazed.

D. Ask and answer. Ask questions about the picture above.

Did he say he was sad?   Yes, he did.   No, he didn't.
Did they say they were amazed?   Yes, they did.   No, they didn't.

Let's Read

A. Read the new words.

| know how to | somersault | trampoline |
| am able to | trapeze | handstand | acrobatics |

B. Read.

Welcome to Maya's Homepage

I'm having a lot of fun at circus camp.

At first, everything was hard. I dropped the balls in juggling class. I wasn't strong. I didn't know how to do a somersault.

Now, I'm stronger. I can do somersaults on the trampoline! I am able to swing on the trapeze. I am able to do a handstand, but I can't stay up. I can juggle three balls easily. I'm one of the best students in the acrobatics class.

We're going to have a circus show at the end of camp. It will be next Saturday. I hope you will be able to come!

C. Choose the best title.

    a. At the Circus
    b. Circus Camp
    c. Trapeze, Trampoline, and Juggling

D. Answer the questions.

1. Where is Maya now?
2. At first, was everything easy or hard?
3. Is Maya able to do a handstand?
4. Is she stronger now?
5. How many balls can she juggle?
6. When is the circus show going to be?

E. Understand the vocabulary.

> I am able to do a handstand, but I can't stay up.

What does am able to mean?
    a. can
    b. did not want
    c. did not like

F. Understand the grammar.

> I can juggle three balls easily.

Which sentence has about the same meaning?
    a. I am able to juggle three balls.
    b. I am not able to juggle three balls.

G. Your turn.

Think of two questions about the reading. Ask your partner.

H. What about you?

Have you ever been to a circus?
Would you like to go to a circus camp?

Let's Build

A. Practice the grammar chant.

The circus was amazing.
I was amazed.
The acrobats were frightening,
But they weren't frightened.

Grandma thought it was boring.
She was really bored,
But the kids said it was exciting.
They were very excited!

B. Make sentences.

He was excited by the horseback ride.   The horseback ride was exciting.

1. excited / horseback ride

2. bored / TV show

3. tired / soccer game

4. frightened / movie

C. Play a game. What did they say?

She said she was happy.   He said the cookies were delicious.

- He was happy.
- The cookies were delicious.
- She was bored.
- They were surprised.
- They went to the circus yesterday.
- They woke up at 6:30 am.
- The movie was interesting.
- They went to the museum.
- The tennis game was exciting.
- The party was amazing.

Who's next?   It's your turn.   It's Kate's turn.
Too bad.   Try again.   Maybe next time.

Units 1-2 Listen and Review

A. Listen and circle.

1.

  a   b   c

2.

  a   b   c

3.

  a   b   c

4.

  a   b   c

B. Listen and check. What did they say?

1. ☐ I was amazed.
   ☐ It was amazing.

2. ☐ It was disappointing.
   ☐ I was disappointed.

C. Listen and circle.

1.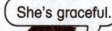

  a   b

2.

  a   b

Let's Read About the Secret Message

"Hi, Everett."
"Hi, JJ."
"What are you doing?" asked JJ.
"I'm trying to read this message," said Everett. "I think my father wrote it."
"Why is the note in code?" asked JJ. "Isn't English easier?"
"My parents use codes to write secret messages," said Everett.
"You like codes," said JJ. "Can you read this one?"
"Sure. This is a substitution code," said Everett. "Look at each letter. Write the letter before it in the alphabet. So *Ij* is *Hi.*"
"Oh, I see," said JJ. "So, *fwfsfuu* is *Everett.* It says *Hi, Everett.*"
"That's right. Let's see what it says."

Ij, Fwfsfuu!
Uifsf bsf tpebt boe tobdlt jo uif sfgsjhfsbups gps zpv boe KK.
Ebe.

"Oh," said JJ. "I see my name there—*KK* instead of *JJ.* I'll get the snacks and sodas!"

New Words
message
secret
instead of
code
substitution
snacks

Hi, Everett!
There are sodas and snacks in the refrigerator for you and JJ.
Dad

↑ ↑ ↑ ↑ ↑ ↑ ↑ ↑
I j, F w f s f u u !
H i E v e r e t t

Unit 3 Going Shopping

Let's Start

A. Let's talk.

Kate: Hi, Andy. What are you doing here?
Andy: I'm buying a birthday present for my mother. What should I get for her?
Kate: What did you buy her last year?
Andy: I bought her a necklace. Should I get her another necklace this year?

Kate: I don't think so. You should get her something different.
Andy: Do you have any ideas?
Kate: Hmmm, there are so many choices. You could get her a teapot. You could get her a cookbook. Does she like to cook?
Andy: Yes, but she already has a lot of cookbooks.

Kate: Does she like scarves? You could get her a scarf.
Andy: These scarves are beautiful. This one is her favorite color.
Kate: Good! And they're on sale! I think you should get her that scarf.
Andy: I think you're right. She'll love it!

B. Let's practice.

| Should I get her a necklace this year? | I think you should. I don't think so. |

get = buy
got = bought

C. Practice the words and sentences.

1. a scarf
2. a necklace
3. a bracelet
4. a box of chocolates

5. a skateboard
6. a cookbook
7. a DVD
8. a watch

I bought a scarf for her last year.   I bought her a scarf last year.

D. Ask and answer.

What could she get her grandmother?   She could get her a necklace or a scarf.

1. grandmother
2. grandfather

3. uncle
4. aunt

Let's Learn

 What did he do?
He bought her a DVD.

A. Practice the words.

1. buy her a DVD

2. send her a postcard

3. give him a package

4. show him a picture

5. print her a picture

6. sell her a watch

B. Practice the sentences.

He **bought her a DVD**.
He **bought a DVD for her**.

buy → bought	send → sent
give → gave	show → showed
print → printed	sell → sold

C. Practice the question and answer.

What did she do?   She **bought him a DVD**.

buy a DVD   print a picture
give a package   sell a bracelet
show a picture   send a package

D. Ask and answer. Ask questions about the picture above.

Did she **buy him a DVD**?   Yes, she did.   No, she didn't.

Let's Read

A. Read the new words.

| plan | alarm clock | yell |
| surprise | | college |

B. Read.

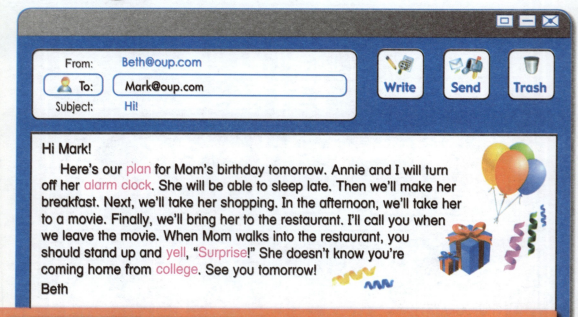

From: Beth@oup.com
To: Mark@oup.com
Subject: Hi!

Hi Mark!

    Here's our plan for Mom's birthday tomorrow. Annie and I will turn off her alarm clock. She will be able to sleep late. Then we'll make her breakfast. Next, we'll take her shopping. In the afternoon, we'll take her to a movie. Finally, we'll bring her to the restaurant. I'll call you when we leave the movie. When Mom walks into the restaurant, you should stand up and yell, "Surprise!" She doesn't know you're coming home from college. See you tomorrow!

Beth

24 Unit 3 / Going Shopping

C. Choose the best title.

    a. Mark's Plans
    b. Mom's Birthday
    c. Beth Goes to the Movies

D. Answer the questions.

1. When is their mother's birthday?
2. Who is coming to the restaurant?
3. Who is Mark?
4. Does Mark live at home?
5. Are Beth and Mark going to cook dinner for their mother?

E. Understand the vocabulary.

> When Mom walks into the restaurant, you should stand up and yell, "Surprise!"

What does yell mean?
    a. talk quietly
    b. talk loudly
    c. talk quickly

F. Understand the grammar.

> I'll call you when we leave the movie.

Which sentence has about the same meaning?
    a. I'm going to call you before we go to the movie.
    b. I'm going to call you after we leave the movie.

G. Your turn.

Think of two questions about the readings. Ask your partner.

H. What about you?

Have you ever planned a surprise birthday party for someone? Who was it for? What did you do?

Let's Build

A. Practice the grammar chant.

I need a present for my mother.
What should I get her?
   How about a necklace?
She doesn't like jewelry.
   You could buy a nice T-shirt.
She doesn't wear T-shirts.
   You could give her a tennis racket.
She hates tennis.
   You could make her a birthday cake.
I can't cook.
   You should take her out to dinner!
Great idea! She'll love it!

B. Make sentences. Ask and answer.

> He could get her a music player or a camera.
> What should he get her?   He should get her a camera.

1. music player / camera

2. watch / fishing pole

3. book / T-shirt

4. tennis racket / dog

5. baseball / DVD

6. watch / wallet

C. Practice the questions and answers.

What should she do?   She should give her teacher a picture.
What shouldn't she do?   She shouldn't give her teacher an apple.

1.

2.

3.

4.

5.

6.

D. Ask and answer. Ask questions about the pictures above.

What did she do?   She gave her teacher a picture.

Unit 4 Around Town

 ## Let's Start

A. Let's talk.

Jenny: Where's the bookstore? Do you see it?
Kate: No, I don't. Should we ask someone?
Jenny: That's a good idea.
Kate: Let's ask that police officer.

Jenny: Excuse me, officer.
Officer: Yes?
Jenny: We're looking for the bookstore. Is it near here?
Officer: Yes, it is. It's over there on the corner.
Jenny: On the corner? Where?
Officer: It's next to the bakery.
Jenny: Oh, now I see it. Thank you.

Clerk: Hello, girls. Can I help you?
Kate: No, thank you. We're just looking.
Jenny: Can we bring our drinks inside?
Clerk: Yes, you can.
Kate: Thank you.

B. Let's practice.

| Can we bring our drinks inside? | Yes, you can. |
| | No, you can't. |

28 Unit 4 / Around Town

C. Practice the words.

1. on the corner

2. across the street

3. over there

4. between

5. around the corner

6. next to

D. Practice the questions and answers.

Where's the bank?
It's over there.
It's next to the library.
It's between the library and the bakery.

Where's the clinic?
It's on the corner.
It's across the street from the school.
It's around the corner from the train station.

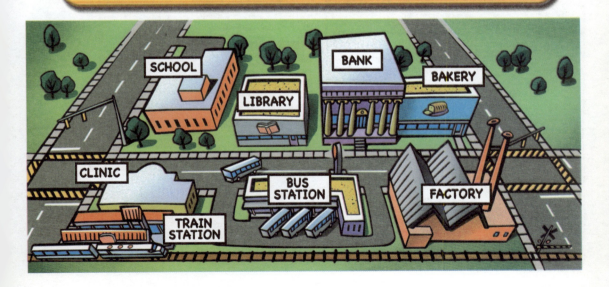

Unit 4 / Around Town

Let's Learn

 How do I get to the park?
Go two blocks and turn right.

A. Say these.

1. Go straight.

2. Go to the corner.

3. Turn left.

4. Turn right.

5. Go two blocks.

6. Cross the street.

B. Practice the directions.

Go straight. Cross the street. Turn right.

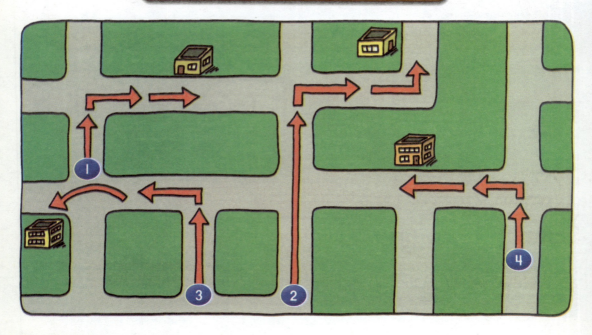

C. Ask and answer. Give directions.

How do I get to the park?   Go two blocks and turn right.

1. park

2. DVD store

3. restaurant

4. airport

5. bank

6. bookstore

7. pet store

8. bakery

Unit 4 / Around Town

Let's Read

A. Read the new words.

| shout ⟶ shouted | from under | bush | directions |
| GPS device (Global Positioning System) | | geocache | location |

B. Read.

TREASURE HUNT

"We found it!" Kristen and Nick Johnson shouted. They pulled the treasure box from under the bush and opened it. Kristen and Nick are playing a game with the help of a machine for maps and directions called a GPS device (Global Positioning System).

The game is to find a geocache, the treasure's hiding place, using a GPS device. There are more than 250,000 geocache locations around the world. Someone fills a box with toys or other treasure. They hide the box and put its GPS location on a list on the website. Treasure hunters use the website and the GPS device to look for the box. It may not always be easy to find, but it is fun to try.

"I like finding treasure," said Kristen.
"I like seeing new places," said Nick.

C. Choose another title.

    a. Treasure Is Everywhere
    b. Hunting for Treasure at Home
    c. How to Play a Treasure Hunt Game

D. Answer the questions.

1. What did Nick and Kristen find?
2. Where did they find it?
3. How did they find it?
4. Is it easy to find a treasure?
5. Do people use a GPS device to hunt for treasure?

E. Understand the vocabulary.

> "We found it!" Kristen and Nick Johnson shouted.

What does shouted mean?
    a. talked quietly
    b. talked fast
    c. talked loudly

F. Understand the grammar.

> They pulled the box from under the bush and opened it.

Which sentence has about the same meaning?
    a. They found the box under the bush. They picked it up and opened it.
    b. They found the box next to the bush and opened it.

G. Your turn.

Think of two questions about the reading. Ask your partner.

H. What about you?

Would you like to look for a geocache?
Where would you hide a treasure?

Let's Build

A. Practice the grammar chant. CD 1 68

I'm looking for Joe. Where did he go?
   I think he went to the auto show.
How did he get there?
   I know.
   I saw him walk to the auto show.
   He walked two blocks and then turned right.
   He stopped for a minute at the traffic light.
   He crossed the street when the light turned green.
   Then he stopped on the corner to talk to Eileen.
   He said, "Eileen, come on, let's go."
   Then they went straight to the auto show.

B. Ask and answer. CD 1 69

What did Tom do first?   He went straight.

1. first / went
2. second / turned
3. third / crossed
4. next / stopped
5. last / talked

34 Unit 4 / Around Town

C. Practice the questions and answers.

Where did he go? He went to the bookstore.
Who did she talk to? She talked to Alan.
Where did they stop? They stopped on the corner.
How many blocks did she walk? She walked two blocks.

D. Ask and answer. Ask questions about the pictures above.

Did he go to the bookstore?   Yes, he did.   No, he didn't.

Units 3-4   Listen and Review

A. Listen and circle. CD1 72

1.
   a   b   c

2.
   a   b   c

3.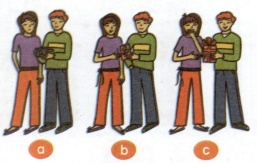
   a   b   c

4.
   a   b   c

B. Listen and check. CD1 73

1.

2.

3.

4.

5.

36   Units 3–4 Listen and Review

Let's Read About the Text Message

"Where's Olivia?" asked Everett. "We were going to meet here at 5 p.m."
"Maybe she's lost," said JJ. "Did you tell her which theater?"
"Yes, I did," said Everett. "I told her to meet us at the theater next to the shopping mall."
"I have a message," said JJ.

"Maybe it's from Olivia," said Everett.
"It is from her. It's a text message. Look." JJ showed Everett her phone.

New Words
ticket   text
prefer   a while

IM L8 = I'm Late
PLS = Please
W8 = wait
4ME = for me
C = See
U = you
L8R = Later

JJ laughed. "Sounds like Olivia, doesn't it?"
"I can't read that," said Everett.
"Sure you can. Just try."
"Oh, I see," said Everett. "It's a code."

"Haven't you ever sent a text message?" asked JJ.
"No, I haven't," said Everett. "I prefer to talk on the phone."
"Well, here," said JJ. She gave her phone to Everett. "You can send a message, and I'll go get some popcorn."
"That's a good idea," said Everett. "We'll probably be waiting for a while. She's always late."

Unit 5 Explore the World

 ## Let's Start

A. Let's talk.

Scott: Have you met Anh? She's the girl who is staying with Sarah's family.
Andy: No, I haven't. She's from Vietnam, isn't she?
Scott: Yes, she is. She's Vietnamese.
Andy: What is she like?
Scott: She is really nice.

Andy: Does she speak English?
Scott: Yes, she does. She speaks Vietnamese and a little English.
Andy: I'd like to meet her.
Scott: O.K. Let's go.

Andy: Hi, Anh. Are you enjoying your home stay?
Anh: Yes, I am. Have you ever been on a home stay?
Andy: No, I haven't.
Anh: You should come to Vietnam and stay with my family.
Andy: Thanks! That sounds like fun.

B. Let's practice.

Have you met Anh?	Yes, I have.
	No, I haven't.

When you go on a home stay, you go to a different country. You live with a family for a short time.

C. Practice the words. Ask and answer.

She's from Australia, isn't she?   Yes, she is. She's Australian.
No, she isn't. She's Thai.

D. What about you?

What country are you from?

Let's Learn

 What language is spoken in Brazil?
Portuguese is spoken in Brazil.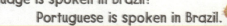

A. Practice the words. (CD 2 06)

1. Brazil
2. Portuguese — Bom dia!
3. black beans
4. France
5. French — Bonjour!
6. croissants
7. Italy
8. Italian — Buongiorno!
9. spaghetti

B. Practice the sentences. Use the pictures above. (CD 2 07) (CD 2 08)

People in Brazil speak Portuguese.
Portuguese is spoken in Brazil.
People in Brazil eat black beans.
Black beans are eaten in Brazil.

speak → is / are spoken
eat → is / are eaten

40 Unit 5 / Explore the World

C. Practice the questions and answers.

What language is spoken in Vietnam? What foods are eaten in Vietnam?
Vietnamese is spoken in Vietnam. Noodles and rice are eaten in Vietnam.

1. Vietnamese / noodles and rice   2. Italian / spaghetti and ravioli

3. Spanish / tacos and burritos   4. English / steak and potatoes

D. What about you?

What languages are spoken in your country?
What foods are eaten in your country?

Let's Read

A. Read the new words.

| cacao | bitter | spicy | the Spanish | sugar |
| Europe | pastries | create → created | | cheaper |

B. Read.

Chocolate

Do you like chocolate? You should thank the Mexicans. Ancient Mexican people made a chocolate drink from cacao seeds. Their chocolate was bitter and spicy. Many years later, cacao seeds were brought to Spain by the Spanish. Spanish people added sugar to their chocolate. This sweet chocolate became the most popular drink in Europe. Both cacao and sugar were very expensive, so only rich people drank chocolate.

Over the years, chocolate was used in cakes and pastries, and in the 1800s, the chocolate candy bar was created. Chocolate also became cheaper, so more people were able to eat and drink it.

C. Choose another title.

    a. Chocolate is Old
    b. Expensive Chocolate
    c. The History of Chocolate

D. True or false?

1. The Spanish made the first chocolate.
2. The first chocolate was a candy bar.
3. The Spanish liked sweet chocolate.
4. People in Europe didn't like sweet chocolate.
5. Chocolate became cheaper.
6. Few people are able to eat chocolate now.

E. Understand the vocabulary.

> Over the years chocolate was used in cakes and pastries, and in the 1880's, the chocolate bar was created.

What does created mean?
    a. cooked
    b. mixed
    c. made

F. Understand the grammar.

> Both cacao and sugar were very expensive, so only rich people drank chocolate.

Which sentence has about the same meaning?
    a. Only rich people drank chocolate, so it was expensive.
    b. Only rich people drank chocolate because it was expensive.

G. Your turn.

Think of two questions about the reading. Ask your partner.

H. What about you?

Do you like chocolate? What's your favorite kind of chocolate?

Let's Build

A. Practice the grammar chant.

Have you met Alice?
She was born in Dallas.
But now she goes to school in Brazil.
Does she speak Portuguese?
Yes, she does.
English is not spoken in her school.

Have you met Maria?
She was born in Korea.
But her mother was born in Rome.
Her father's Korean.
Her mother's Italian.
And Korean is spoken at home.

안녕

Bom dia!

B. Make sentences.

The money was found by Mark.
The money was found.

found → found	broke → broken
lost → lost	drew → drawn
bought → bought	rented → rented

1. Kelly found the money.

2. Mark broke the window.

3. Tina lost the cell phone.

4. Jodie drew the picture.

5. Jason bought the camera.

6. Sam rented the DVD.

C. Make sentences.

> The alarm was set

| set → set | ate → eaten |
| painted → painted | made → made |

1.
2.
3.
4.
5.
6.

D. Ask and answer. Ask questions about the pictures above.

> What happened?   Someone set the alarm.

Unit 6 Doing Things

Let's Start

A. Let's talk.

Andy: Who's she?
Jenny: She's my aunt.
Andy: Where was this picture taken?
Jenny: That was taken in Rome. She's moving there!

Andy: Really? Right now?
Jenny: No, she hasn't moved yet. She still lives in London.
Andy: How long has she lived there?
Jenny: She has lived there since last January.

Andy: She has lived in London for three months, and she's moving again?
Jenny: She moves a lot because she's a pilot.
Andy: Wow! That's exciting! I want to be a pilot, too!

Did You Know?
for = amount of time (for five years)
since = starting time (since last January)

B. Let's practice.

Has she already moved?   Yes, she has already moved.
                         No, she hasn't moved yet.

C. Practice the words. Ask and answer.

> He is → He has been
> He teaches → He has taught
> He lives → He has lived
> He studies → He has studied
> He has → He has had

1. been at the hotel since yesterday evening

2. studied English since last year

3. lived in New York since last summer

4. had a cold for two days

5. taught French for three months

6. been friends for a long time

How long has he been at the hotel?
He has been at the hotel since yesterday evening.

since	for
2006	three years
Monday	four days
June	five months
4:00 p.m.	30 minutes
last summer	a long time
yesterday	a few days
early evening	an hour

D. What about you?

How long have you studied English?

Let's Learn

How long has he been doing homework?
He has been doing homework for two hours.

A. Practice the words. CD 2 21

1. practicing the piano for 30 minutes

2. doing homework since two o'clock

3. cleaning his room for three hours

4. talking on the phone since early evening

5. playing soccer for two and a half hours

6. visiting Hong Kong since last week

B. Practice the sentences. CD 2 22 CD 2 23

> She has been practicing the piano for 30 minutes.
> They've been visiting Hong Kong since last week.

48 Unit 6 / Doing Things

C. Practice the question and answer.

> How long has he been doing homework?
> He has been doing homework for two hours.
> How long have they been practicing soccer?
> They've been practicing soccer since 3:00.

1. two hours

2. last Thursday

3. 3:00

4. fifteen minutes

5. noon

6. three and a half hours

Let's Read

A. Read the new words.

| Colorado | homesick | neighbor | Seven Summits |
| continents | camp → camped | promise → promised |

B. Read.

Welcome to Johnny's Homepage

I've been on a home stay in Colorado for three months. I'm not homesick anymore! My English has gotten better, and I'm making new friends.

Mt. Everest, Asia, 29,029 feet
Mt. Aconcagua, South America, 22,841 feet
Mt. Denali, North America, 20,322 feet
Mt. Kilimanjaro, Africa, 19,341 feet
Mt. Elbrus, Europe, 18,510 feet
Mt. Vinson Massif, 16,050 feet
Carstensz Pyramid, Australia, 16,024 feet

One of my new friends is Alex. He's my neighbor. Alex climbs mountains. He has climbed the Seven Summits. Those are the highest mountains on the seven continents. He took me mountain climbing last weekend. We hiked up a mountain on Saturday night and camped. Then we hiked down on Sunday. Alex said I was a good climber. I really like mountain climbing! Alex has promised to take me with him next time, too.

C. Choose the best title.

a. Johnny Isn't Homesick Anymore
b. Johnny's Mountain Climbing Adventure
c. The Seven Summits

D. Answer the questions.

1. How long has Johnny been on a home stay?
2. Has he been homesick?
3. Who is Alex?
4. Which mountains has Alex climbed?
5. Did Johnny and Alex climb the Seven Summits?

E. Understand the vocabulary.

> Alex has promised to take me with him next time, too.

What does promised mean?
a. Alex will take Johnny.
b. Maybe Alex will take Johnny.
c. Alex will not take Johnny.

F. Understand the grammar.

> He has climbed the Seven Summits. Those are the highest mountains on the seven continents.

Which sentence has about the same meaning?
a. He has climbed seven mountains.
b. He has climbed the seven highest mountains on the seven continents.

G. Your turn.

Think of two questions about the reading.
Ask your partner.

H. What about you?

Have you ever been mountain climbing?
Would you like to go?

Let's Build

A. Practice the grammar chant.

How long have you been waiting for Ken?
 I've been waiting for Ken since ten.

How long has he been talking to Sue?
 He's been talking to Sue since two.

How long has Anne been taking a bath?
 She's been taking a bath for an hour and a half.

How long have you been studying with Ray?
 I started yesterday.

B. Make sentences.

She has been swimming for 30 minutes.   He has lived in Bangkok since 2006.

1. swimming
   30 minutes

2. had a cold
   two days

3. writing an e-mail
   8:00

4. lived in Bangkok
   2006

5. riding her bicycle
   an hour and a half

6. studied Spanish
   last spring

C. Make sentences.

> He has already walked the dog.   He hasn't walked the dog yet.

1. walked the dog

2. washed her hands

3. cleaned her room

4. done his homework

5. fed the dog

6. taken a bath

7. eaten dinner

8. gone shopping

D. Ask and answer. Ask questions about the pictures above.

> Has he walked the dog yet?   Yes, he has.   No, he hasn't.

Unit 6 / Doing Things

Units 5-6   Listen and Review

A. Listen and circle.

1.
   a   b

2.
   a   b

3.
   a   b

4.
   a   b

B. Listen and check.

1. ☐ Portuguese is spoken in Brazil.
   ☐ People in Brazil speak Portuguese.

2. ☐ Ravioli is eaten in Italy.
   ☐ People in Italy eat ravioli.

3. ☐ People in France speak French.
   ☐ French is spoken in France.

4. ☐ Rice is eaten in Vietnam.
   ☐ People in Vietnam eat rice.

C. Listen and check.

1.
   ☐ She has been practicing the piano for 45 minutes.
   ☐ He has been practicing the piano since yesterday.

2.
   ☐ She has lived in Paris for two years.
   ☐ She has been visiting Paris for two weeks.

3. ☐ She has taught Spanish since last spring.
   ☐ He has taught Spanish for two years.

4. ☐ She has been talking since 3:00.
   ☐ She has been talking since 3:30.

Let's Read About the Hidden Gold

"What's this?" asked JJ. "It doesn't look like English."
"It's mirror writing," said Everett. "The writing is backward."
"What does it say?" asked JJ.
"I don't know. I'll get a mirror." Everett returned with a mirror. "Look at this," said Everett.

I found the gold behind the middle stone of the fireplace. Oh, I am a silly fool!

"Gold!" said JJ. "Do you think it's in your fireplace?"

"I don't know," said Everett. "Let's go and look. Maybe the gold is still there."
They ran inside and moved the stone. JJ pulled out a bag. Inside, there were shiny, gold rocks. Everett laughed.
"Look!" JJ said. "Gold."
"It's not gold," Everett said. "It's Fool's Gold. Remember the words, *I am a silly fool*?"
"Isn't it gold?" asked JJ.
"No, it isn't," said Everett. "Someone hid these stones a long time ago. It was a game."
"Someone found the stones," said JJ.
"Then they put them back."
"So we could find them," said Everett.
"Now we're silly fools, too!"

New Words
return →	returned
silly	backward
fireplace	stone
gold	Fool's Gold

Unit 7 About Me

Let's Start

A. Let's talk. (CD 2 36)

Kate: Look at this picture. Is that you?
Scott: Yes, it is. I was two in that picture.
Kate: Could you swim when you were two?
Scott: Yes, I could. I learned how to swim before I was able to walk.

Kate: When did you learn how to swim?
Scott: I learned how to swim when I was one year old.
Kate: That's really young!
Scott: My mother taught me. I've always loved the water.

Scott: When did you learn how to swim?
Kate: I've never learned how. I couldn't swim when I was one, and I can't swim now.
Scott: My mom can teach you. She's a good teacher.
Kate: Thanks. I'd like that.

B. Let's practice. (CD 2 37)

Could you swim when you were two?
Yes, I could.   No, I couldn't.

can → could
am able to → was able to

C. Practice the words. Ask and answer.

> When did she learn how to walk?
> She learned how to walk when she was one year old.

1. learn how to walk

2. learn how to write his name

3. learn how to read

4. learn how to ride a bicycle

5. learn how to swim

6. learn how to ice skate

7. learn how to do a handstand

8. learn how to ski

D. What about you?

When did you learn how to ride a bicycle?

Let's Learn

 What are they like? They're usually outgoing, but sometimes they're shy.

A. Practice the words. CD 2 40

1. outgoing

2. shy

3. generous

4. selfish

5. studious

6. lazy

B. Practice the sentences. CD 2 41 CD 2 42

Amy and Brad are outgoing. They're outgoing people.

Amy, Lisa, and Sarah = they
Amy and I = we

C. Practice the question and answer.

> What are they like?   They're usually outgoing, but sometimes they're shy.

1. outgoing / shy

2. generous / selfish

3. studious / lazy

4. studious / selfish

5. generous / shy

6. outgoing / lazy

D. What about you?

What are you like?
I'm usually _____, but sometimes I'm _____.

Let's Read

A. Read the new words.

| introduce | team | athletic |
| perfect | generally | |

B. Read.

Personality Quiz

1 There is a new student in your class. What will you do?
  a. Introduce the student to my friends.
  b. Ask the student to join my sports team.
  c. Listen to everything the student says.

2 What do you like to do in your free time?
  a. Go out with a lot of friends.
  b. Be outside and play sports.
  c. Stay home and read, or listen to music.

3 What's your idea of a perfect party?
  a. Have a big party at a restaurant.
  b. Have a party at a roller skating rink.
  c. Have a small party at home with three or four friends.

4 What do you like best about school?
  a. Seeing and talking to my friends.
  b. Playing sports.
  c. Learning new things and listening to my classmates.

a = 3 points   b = 2 points

Answers:
4-6 points = You're generally shy and like listening to other people.

7-9 points = You're generally athletic and like doing things with other people.

10-12 points = You're generally outgoing and like talking to other people.

C. Choose the best title.

a. Who Are You?
b. What Are You Like?
c. Are You Outgoing or Shy?

D. True or false?

1. An outgoing person generally likes to talk to other people.
2. A shy person generally likes to meet new people.
3. An athletic person generally likes to play outdoors.
4. A shy person wouldn't like a small party.
5. A kind person likes to help people.
6. An outgoing person wouldn't like a big party.

E. Understand the vocabulary.

> What's your idea of a perfect party?

What does perfect mean?
a. not good   b. good   c. the best

F. Understand the grammar.

> You are generally athletic and like doing things with other people.

Which sentence has about the same meaning?
a. You like sports and people.
b. You don't like sports, but you like people.

G. Your turn.

Take the quiz with a partner. Compare your answers.

H. What about you?

What's your idea of a perfect day?

Let's Build

A. Practice the grammar chant.

How old were you when you learned to run?
  I was one, I was one.
  I learned to run when I was one.
  I was one when I learned to run.

How old were you when you went to the zoo?
  I was two, I was two.
  I went to the zoo when I was two.
  I was two when I went to the zoo.

How old were you when you learned to ski?
  I was three, I was three.
  I learned to ski when I was three.
  I was three when I learned to ski.

B. Ask your partner.

When did you learn how to swim?   I learned how to swim when I was five.
                                   I was five when I learned how to swim.

	You	Your Partner
1. swim?		
2. ride a bicycle?		
3. write your name in English?		
4. ice skate?		
5. fly a kite?		

C. Make sentences.

| She | was / wasn't | able to ride a bicycle when she was five |

can = is able to
can't = isn't able to
could = was able to
couldn't = wasn't able to

1. ride a bicycle / 5 years old

2. speak English / 4 years old

What's your name?

3. do a somersault / 7 years old

4. fly a kite / 4 years old

5. play the piano / 6 years old

6. ice skate / 9 years old

D. Ask and answer. Ask questions about the pictures above.

Could she ride a bicycle when she was five?   Yes, she could.
                                               No, she couldn't.

Unit 8 In the Future

Let's Start

A. Let's talk.

Andy: I'd like to visit the Amazon jungle someday.
Kate: Why?
Andy: Because I'd like to see a rainforest.
Kate: What would you do there?
Andy: I'd look at the plants and animals.

Andy: What would you like to do in the future?
Kate: I'd like to climb Mt. Everest.
Andy: Why? What would you do at the top?
Kate: I'd stand there. I think it would be fun to stand on the highest mountain.
Andy: I don't think so.

Kate: If you ever go to the rainforest, send me a postcard.
Andy: I will, and remember to send me a postcard from Mt. Everest.
Kate: I promise.

B. Let's practice.

I think it would be fun.   I don't think it would be fun.

C. Practice the words. Ask and answer.

1. visit the Amazon jungle

2. climb Mt. Everest

3. dive to the bottom of the ocean

4. see the pyramids of Egypt

5. ride an elephant

6. travel to the moon

What would you like to do someday?   I'd like to visit the Amazon jungle.

D. What about you?

What would you like to do someday?

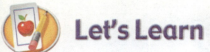 **Let's Learn**

 If you could go anywhere, where would you go? 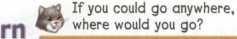 I'd go to Hawaii!

A. Practice the words.

1. go to Antarctica

2. go to Mars

3. meet a TV star

4. meet a sports star

5. buy a pony

6. buy a motorbike

7. go kayaking

8. go skydiving

B. Practice the sentences.

If I could go anywhere, I'd go to Antarctica.
If I could meet anyone, I'd meet a TV star.
If I could buy anything, I'd buy a pony.
If I could do anything, I'd go kayaking.

Unit 8 / In the Future

C. Practice the questions and answers.

> If you could go anywhere, where would you go?
> I'd go to Hawaii.

anyone = who
anywhere = where
anything = what

1. go to Hawaii

2. go surfing

3. meet a rock star

4. buy a car

5. meet a movie director

6. go to London

D. Practice the grammar chant.

If you could do anything, what would you do?
   I'd climb Mt. Everest from Katmandu.
I would, if I could.
I would if I could, but I can't.

If you could speak any language, what would you speak?
   I'd speak French, English, Japanese, and Greek.
I would, if I could.
I would if I could, but I can't.

If you could buy anything, what would you buy?
   I'd buy a little plane and learn to fly.
I would, if I could.
I would if I could, but I can't.

Unit 8 / In the Future

Let's Read

A. Read the new words. 🔊 CD 2 61

| Alaska | glaciers | Galapagos Islands | giant tortoises |
| Mayan | Kenya | wild | India | Taj Mahal |

If you could go anywhere, where would you go?

B. Read. 🔊 CD 2 62

I'd like to go to Alaska. I'd love to ski there. There are also a lot of glaciers in Alaska. I've never seen one before, but I'd like to.

I'd go to the Galapagos Islands. I've heard they have penguins and giant tortoises there. I'd like to see those!

I'd go to Mexico and see the Mayan pyramids. I've seen the pyramids in Egypt, but I'd like to see the Mayan pyramids, too.

I'd go to India. I love hot, spicy food, and I like Indian music. I'd also like to see the Taj Mahal.

I'd go to Kenya to see wild animals and take pictures of them. I've seen animals in a zoo, but I'd like to see wild animals in their homes.

C. Choose the best title.

    a. Things I'd Like to See
    b. Places I'd Like to Go
    c. Food I'd Like to Eat

D. Answer the questions.

1. Where can you see giant tortoises?
2. What can you do in Alaska?
3. Where can you visit the Taj Mahal?
4. Which two countries have pyramids?
5. In which two countries can you see wild animals?

E. Understand the vocabulary.

> There are a lot of glaciers in Alaska.

What is a glacier made of?
    a. rocks
    b. water
    c. snow

F. Understand the grammar.

> I've never seen one before, but I'd like to.

Which sentence has about the same meaning?
    a. I've never seen Alaska before, but I'd like to.
    b. I've never seen a glacier before, but I'd like to.

G. Your turn.

Think of two questions about the reading. Ask your partner.

H. What about you?

If you could go anywhere, where would you go?
Why? What would you do?

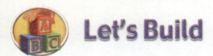

Let's Build

A. Play a game.

Roll a die. Move your marker. Follow the directions in the box at the top of page 71.

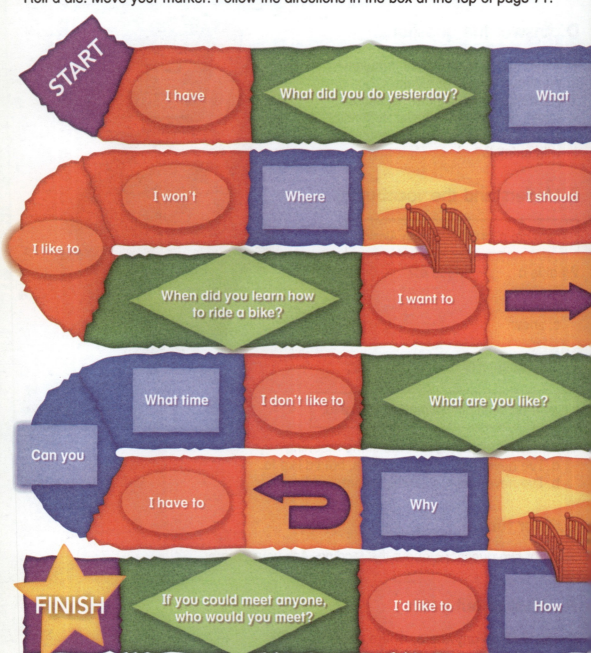

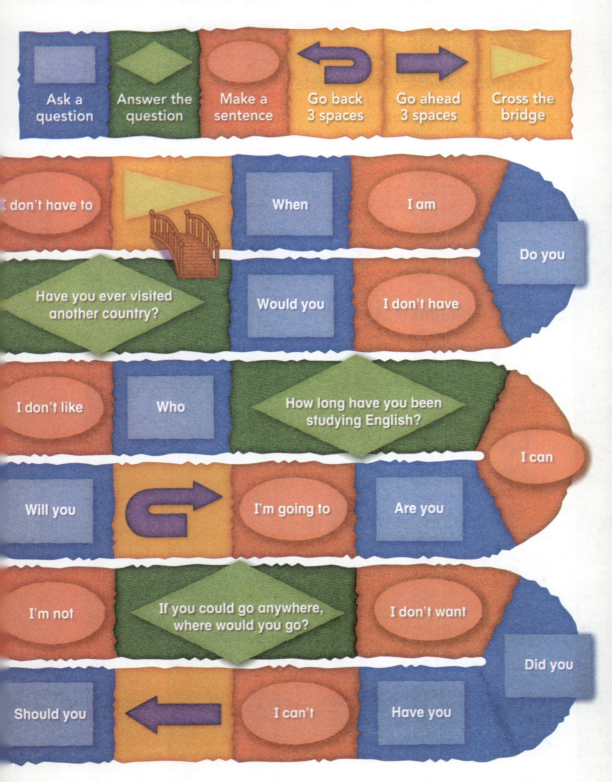

Units 7-8 Listen and Review

A. Listen and check. True or false? (CD 2, 63)

1. He would like to visit Mars.
   ☐ True ☐ False

2. She would like to go to Hawaii.
   ☐ True ☐ False

3. He would like to meet a rock star.
   ☐ True ☐ False

4. She would climb Mt. Everest.
   ☐ True ☐ False

5. She would like to go to Mexico and visit the pyramids.
   ☐ True ☐ False

6. He would like to meet a soccer star.
   ☐ True ☐ False

B. Listen and number. (CD 2, 64)

1. Amy learned how to walk

2. Brad learned how to do a handstand

3. Nick wasn't able to ride a bicycle

4. Jackie was able to do a somersault

5. Sam and Brian were outgoing

a. when he was four.

☐ b. when they were young.

☐ c. when she was one.

☐ d. when she was six.

☐ e. when he was ten.

Let's Read About the Surprise Party

"What's wrong, Everett? You look puzzled. You shouldn't look puzzled on your birthday," said JJ.
"I am puzzled," said Everett. "My mother gave me this birthday card, and I can't figure it out."
"Let me see." JJ looked at the card. "Can't you read the code?"
"Oh, that part is easy," said Everett. "I don't understand the numbers."

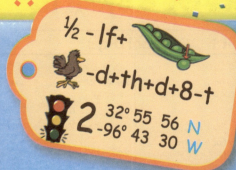

"Hmmm," said JJ. "N could be North, and W could be West."
"So?"
"I think these show latitude and longitude."
"How do they help me find the place?" asked Everett.
"It's simple." JJ opened a website on her computer. "We type in the numbers and press the button."

New Words
puzzled — figure it out
North — West
latitude — longitude
website — city
zoom — neighborhood

"Look at the map!" said Everett.
"That's our city."
"Now we zoom in," said JJ.
"That's our neighborhood," said Everett.
"And we zoom in some more," said JJ.
"That's the park," said Everett. "Why does it show our park?"
"Come on," said JJ. "Let's go and see!"
They raced to the park.

"Surprise!"
"Happy Birthday, Everett," said JJ.
"Wow!" said Everett. "This is great! Thanks."

Let's Go 6 Syllabus

Unit 1 — School Days

Let's Start

Whose hat is that?
It's Anna's hat. It's hers.
Asking and answering questions about possessions

It's my hat. = It's mine.
It's your hat. = It's yours.
Talking about possessions

Which girl is Anna?
She's the girl who is watering the plants.
Identifying people by what they're doing

Let's Learn

He was talking on a cell phone when the bell rang.
When the bell rang, he was talking on a cell phone.
Talking about things happening at the same time

What was he doing when the bell rang?
He was taking a nap.
Asking and answering questions about things happening at the same time

Was he talking on a cell phone when the bell rang?
Yes, he was.
No, he wasn't.
Asking and answering questions about things happening at the same time

Let's Read

The First Ice Pop

Let's Build

Whose jacket is it?
It's Wendy's jacket. It's hers.
Asking about possessions

Bill was reading a book when the doorbell rang.
Talking about things happening at the same time

Which boy is Bill?
He's the boy who is reading a book.
Identifying people by what they're doing

Unit 2 — Weekend Fun

Let's Start

You went to the circus last weekend, didn't you?
Yes, I did.
No, I didn't.
Checking information

The clowns were frightening.
He was frightened.
Describing people and things
Expressing emotions

Let's Learn

The acrobat is beautiful.
He said the acrobat was beautiful.
Reporting what someone else said

What did he say?
He said the acrobat was beautiful.
Asking and telling what someone else said

Did she say she was graceful?
Yes, she did.
No, she didn't.
Asking about what someone else said

Let's Read

Welcome to Maya's Homepage!

Let's Build

He was excited by the circus. The circus was exciting.
Describing people and things
Expressing emotions

She said she was happy.
He said the cookies were delicious.
Reporting what someone else said

Units 1–2 Listen and Review   **Let's Learn About the Secret Message**

Unit 3 — Going Shopping

Let's Start

Should I get her a necklace this year?
I think you should.
I don't think so.
Asking for and giving advice

I bought a scarf for her last year.
I bought her a scarf last year.
Talking about buying gifts for others

What could she get her grandmother?
She could get her a scarf.
Asking about possibilities

Let's Learn

He bought her a DVD.
He bought a DVD for her.
Talking about gifts someone bought

What did she do?
She bought him a DVD.
Asking and talking about what someone did for someone else

Did she buy him a DVD?
Yes, she did.
No, she didn't.
Asking about what someone did for someone else

Let's Read

An Email to Mark

Let's Build

He could get her a music player or a camera. What should he get her?
He should get her a camera.
Giving suggestions
Asking for and giving advice

What should she do?
She should give her teacher a picture.
What shouldn't she do?
She shouldn't give her teacher an apple.
Asking and telling what someone should or shouldn't do

What did she do?
She gave her teacher a picture.
Asking and telling what someone did

Unit 4 — Around Town

Let's Start
Can we bring our drinks inside?
Yes, you can. No, you can't.
Asking for permission

Where's the bank?
It's over there.
It's next to the library.
It's between the library and the bakery.
Asking and telling where places are located

Let's Learn
Go straight. Cross the street.
Turn right.
Giving directions.

How do I get to the park?
Go two blocks and turn right.
Asking for and giving directions

Let's Read
Treasure Hunt

Let's Build
What did Tom do first?
He went straight.
Talking about the order of people's actions

Where did he go?
He went to the bookstore.
Did he go to the bookstore?
Yes, he did.
No, he didn't.
Asking and telling about where people went and what they did

Units 3–4 Listen and Review   **Let's Learn About the Text Message**

Unit 5 — Explore the World

Let's Start
Have you met Ahn?
Yes, I have.
No, I haven't.
Asking and answering if something has happened

She's from Australia, isn't she?
Yes, she is. She's Australian.
No, she isn't. She's Thai.
Checking information

Let's Learn
People in Brazil speak Portuguese.
Portuguese is spoken in Brazil.
People in Brazil eat black beans.
Black beans are eaten in Brazil.
Talking about languages and foods in different countries

What language is spoken in Vietnam?
Vietnamese is spoken in Vietnam.
What foods are eaten in Vietnam?
Noodles and rice are eaten in Vietnam.
Asking and answering about foods and languages in different countries

Let's Read
Chocolate

Let's Build
The money was found by Mark.
The money was found.
The alarm was set.
Talking about things that happened and were done by someone in the past

What happened?
Someone set the alarm.
Asking and answering about what happened

Unit 6 — Doing Things

Let's Start
Has she already moved?
Yes, she has already moved.
No, she hasn't moved yet.
Asking and answering if something has happened or not

How long has he been at the hotel?
He has been at the hotel since yesterday evening.
Asking and answering how long something has been in progress

Let's Learn
She has been practicing the piano for 30 minutes.
They've been visiting Hong Kong since last week.
Talking about how long something has been happening

How long has he been doing homework?
He has been doing homework for two hours.
How long have they been practicing soccer?
They have been practicing soccer since 3:00.
Asking and answering how long something has been happening

Let's Read
Welcome to Johnny's Homepage

Let's Build
He has been swimming for 30 minutes.
She has lived in Bangkok since 2006.
Talking about how long something has been in progress

He has already walked the dog.
He hasn't walked the dog yet.
Talking about if something has happened or not

Has he walked the dog yet?
Yes, he has. No, he hasn't.
Asking and answering if something has happened or not

Units 5–6 Listen and Review   **Let's Learn About the Hidden Gold**

Let's Go 6 Syllabus

Unit 7 — About Me

Let's Start
Could you swim when you were two?
Yes, I could. No, I couldn't.
Asking about when someone could do something

When did she learn how to walk?
She learned how to walk when she was one.
Asking and answering about when someone learned something

Let's Learn
Amy and Brad are outgoing.
They're outgoing people.
Describing people's personalities

What are they like?
They're usually outgoing, but sometimes they're shy.
Asking and answering about people's personalities

Let's Read
Personality Quiz

Let's Build
When did you learn how to swim?
I learned how to swim when I was five.
I was five when I learned how to swim.
Asking and answering when you learned to do something

She was able to ride a bicycle when she was five.
She wasn't able to ride a bicycle when she was five.
Saying when someone could or couldn't do something

Could she ride a bicycle when she was five?
Yes, she could.
No, she couldn't.
Asking and answering when someone could do something

Unit 8 — In the Future

Let's Start
I think it would be fun.
I don't think it would be fun.
Telling someone your opinion

What would you like to do someday?
I'd like to visit the Amazon jungle.
Asking and answering what you would like to do in the future

Let's Learn
If I could go anywhere, I'd go to Antarctica.
If I could meet anyone, I'd meet a TV star.
If I could buy anything, I'd buy a pony.
If I could do anything, I'd go kayaking.
Talking about things you would like to do

If you could go anywhere, where would you go?
I'd go to Hawaii.
Asking and answering about things you would like to do

Let's Read
If You Could Go Anywhere, Where Would You Go?

Let's Build
Play a game.
Making different questions and sentences
Reviewing different question and answer types

Units 7–8 Listen and Review   Let's Learn About the Surprise Party

Teacher and Student Card List Level Six

Unit 1
1. watering the plants
2. feeding the fish
3. writing on the board
4. talking to the teacher
5. reading a textbook
6. writing an essay
7. doing some homework
8. looking for something
9. talking on his cell phone
10. listening to music
11. taking a nap
12. reading a magazine
13. cleaning his room
14. writing a message

Unit 2
15. The acrobats were amazing.
16. She was amazed.
17. Backstage was interesting.
18. He was interested.
19. The clowns were frightening.
20. He was frightened.
21. The juggler was disappointing.
22. She was disappointed.
23. The acrobat is beautiful.
24. The man is strong.
25. The dancers are graceful.
26. The clowns are silly.
27. The T-shirt is expensive.
28. The ice cream is delicious.

Unit 3
29. a scarf
30. a necklace
31. a bracelet
32. a box of chocolates
33. a skateboard
34. a cookbook
35. a DVD
36. a watch
37. grandmother
38. grandfather
39. uncle
40. aunt
41. buy her a DVD
42. send her a postcard
43. give him a package
44. show him a picture
45. print her a picture
46. sell her a watch

Unit 4
47. on the corner
48. across the street
49. over there
50. between
51. around the corner
52. next to
53. go straight
54. go to the corner
55. turn left
56. turn right
57. go two blocks
58. cross the street
59. park
60. DVD store
61. restaurant
62. airport
63. bank
64. bookstore
65. pet store
66. bakery

Unit 5
67. Australia
68. Australian
69. Vietnam
70. Vietnamese
71. Thailand
72. Thai
73. Mexico
74. Mexican
75. Brazil
76. Portuguese
77. black beans
78. France
79. French
80. croissants
81. Italy
82. Italian
83. spaghetti

Unit 6
84. been at the hotel
85. since yesterday evening
86. studied English
87. since last year
88. lived in New York
89. since last summer
90. had a cold
91. for two days
92. taught French
93. for three months
94. been friends
95. for a long time
96. practicing the piano
97. for 30 minutes
98. doing homework
99. since two o'clock
100. cleaning his room
101. for three hours
102. talking on the phone
103. since early evening
104. playing soccer
105. for two and a half hours
106. visiting Hong Kong
107. since last week

Unit 7
108. learn how to walk
109. learn how to write his name
110. learn how to read
111. learn how to ride a bicycle
112. learn how to swim
113. learn how to ice skate
114. learn how to do a handstand
115. learn how to ski
116. outgoing
117. shy
118. generous
119. selfish
120. studious
121. lazy

Unit 8
122. visit the Amazon jungle
123. climb Mt. Everest
124. dive to the bottom of the ocean
125. see the pyramids of Egypt
126. ride an elephant
127. travel to the moon
128. go to Antarctica
129. go to Mars
130. meet a TV star
131. meet a sports star
132. buy a pony
133. buy a motorbike
134. go kayaking
135. go skydiving

Word List

A

a 3
a lot of 20
a while 37
able 14
about 2
acrobatics 14
acrobats 10
across the street 29
added 6
adventure 51
afternoon 24
again 17
airport 31
alarm 45
alarm clock 24
Alaska 68
all 6
alphabet 19
already 20
also 68
always 31
am 14
amazed 10
amazing 10
Amazon jungle 64
amount 46
an 3
an hour and a half 52
ancient 42
and 6
animals 64
another 20
Antarctica 66
any 20
anymore 50
anyone 66
anything 66
anywhere 66
apple 27
are 2
around 6
around the corner 29
asked 19
at 6
athletic 60
aunt 21
Australia 39
Australian 39
auto show 34

B

back 55
backstage 10
backward 55
bad 17
bag 55
bakery 28
balls 10
Bangkok 52
bank 29
baseball 26
bath 52
be 14
beautiful 12

became 42
because 10
bed 6
been 38
before 10
bell 4
best 14
better 50
between 29
bicycle 57
big 60
birthday 20
birthday card 73
bitter 24
black beans 40
blocks 35
board 3
book 9
bookstore 28
bored 16
boring 16
born 44
both 42
bottom of the ocean 65
bought 20
box 31
box of chocolates 21
boy 2
bracelet 21
Brazil 40
breakfast 24
bring 24
broke 44
broken 44
brought 42
burritos 41
bus station 29
bush 31
but 16
button 73
buy 20
buying 20
by 16

C

cacao 42
cake 26
cakes 42
call 24
called 6
camera 26
camp 14
camped 50
can 14
candy bar 42
can't 14
car 67
card 73
cell phone 4
chairs 10
cheaper 42
chocolate 42
choices 20
circus 10
city 73

class 14
classmates 60
cleaned her room 53
cleaning 4
climb 51
climbed 50
climber 50
climbs 50
clinic 29
clowns 10
coat 8
code 19
codes 19
cold 6
college 24
color 20
Colorado 50
come 6
come on 34
coming 24
computer 73
continent 50
continents 50
cook 20
cookbook 20
cookies 17
could 20
couldn't 56
countries 69
country 38
create 42
created 42
croissants 40
cross the street 30
crossed 34
cup 6

D

dance 11
dad 19
Dallas 44
dancers 12
day 61
days 47
delicious 12
did 6
didn't 10
different 20
dinner 25
dinner 25
directions 31
disappointed 11
disappointing 11
dive 65
do 6
does 7
doesn't 24
dog 26
doing 3
done his homework 53
don't 28
doorbell 9
drank 42
drawn 44
drew 44

drink 6
drinks 28
dropped 14
DVD 21
DVD store 31

E

each 19
early 47
easier 19
easily 14
easy 15
eat 9
eaten 40
eaten dinner 53
elephant 65
eleven-year-old 6
end 14
English 19
enjoy 6
enjoying 38
essay 3
Europe 42
evening 47
ever 37
everything 14
everywhere 32
excited 16
exciting 10
exciting 16
excuse me 28
expensive 12

F

face 9
factory 29
family 38
fast 33
father 19
father's 44
favorite 7
fed the dog 53
feeding 3
few 43
fifteen 49
figure it out 73
fills 31
finally 24
find 73
finding 31
fireplace 55
first 6
fish 3
fishing pole 26
five 46
flavor 7
fly 62
food 68
foods 41
fool 55
fools 55
Fool's Gold 55
for 2
forgot 6
found 31

four 47
France 40
free 60
French 40
friends 47
frightened 11
frightening 11
from 24
from under 31
frozen 6
fruit 10
fun 14
funny 10
future 64

G

garden 42
Galapagos Islands 68
game 31
gave 22
generally 60
generous 58
geocache 31
get 19
giant tortoise 68
girl 2
girls 28
give 22
glacier 68
glaciers 68
glove 2
gloves 8
go 38
go straight 30
go to the corner 30
go two blocks 30
goes 44
going 14
gold 55
gone shopping 53
good 20
got 20
gotten 50
GPS device (Global Positioning System) 31
graceful 12
grandfather 21
grandma 16
grandmother 21
great 10
Greek 67
green 34

H

had a cold 52
half 48
handstand 14
happened 7
happy 13
hard 14
has 7
hat 2
hates 26
hats 2

have 14
haven't 37
having 14
Hawaii 67
hello 28
help 28
her 2
here 20
here's 24
hers 2
he's 2
hi 19
hidden 55
hiding place 31
highest 50
hiked 50
his 2
history 7
home 24
home stay 38
homepage 14
homes 68
homesick 50
homework 3
Hong Kong 48
hope 14
hot 68
hotel 47
hour 47
how 7
hunting 32

I

I 2
ice cream 12
ice pop 6
ice pops 7
ice skate 57
I'd 38
idea 26
ideas 20
I'll 19
I'm 14
in 6
India 68
Indian 68
inside 6
instead of 19
interested 11
interesting 11
into 24
introduce 60
invent 6
invented 6
is 2
isn't 2
it 2
Italian 40
Italy 40
it's 2
I've 50

J

jacket 8
January 46

Japanese 67
jeans 8
jewelry 26
join 60
juggle 14
juggled 10
jugglers 10
juggling 14
June 47
just 28

K

Katmandu 67
kayaking 66
Kenya 68
kids 6
kind 43
kite 62
know 6
Korea 44
Korean 44

L

language 41
last 10
last spring 52
late 24
later 37
latitude 73
laughed 37
lazy 58
learn 56
learned 56
leave 7
let's 19
letter 19
library 29
light 34
like 6
list 31
listen 9
listening 4
little 38
live 25
lived 47
lived in Bangkok 52
lives 46
London 46
long 46
longitude 73
look 19
looked 6
looking 2
lost 37
lot 14
loudly 25
love 20
loved 56

M

machine 31
made 42
magazine 4
make 7
making 6

many 7
map 73
maps 31
Mars 66
Mayan 68
maybe 17
meet 37
message 4
met 38
Mexican 39
Mexico 39
middle 55
mine 2
minute 34
mirror 55
mirror writing 55
mittens 2
mix 6
mixed 6
mixing 6
mom 24
mom's 24
Monday 47
money 44
months 46
moon 65
more 42
morning 6
most 42
mother 6
mother's 44
motorbike 66
mountain 50
mountain climbing 50
moved 46
movie 16
movie director 67
moving 46
Mt. Everest 64
museum 17
music 4
music player 26
my 2

N
name 57
nap 4
near 28
necklace 20
neighbor 50
neighborhood 73
never 56
new 31
New York 47
next 14
next to 28
nice 26
night 6
no 2
noodles 41
noon 49
North 73
not 15
note 19
now 14
numbers 73

O
O.K. 38
off 24
officer 28
oh 19
old 43
on 3
on the corner 29
one 6
only 42
opened 31
other 2
our 2
ours 2
out 6
outdoors 61
outgoing 58
outside 6
over 42
over there 28

P
page 24
package 22
painted 45
parents 19
Paris 54
park 31
party 17
pastries 42
penguins 68
people 40
perfect 60
person 61
pet store 31
phone 37
piano 48
picked it up 33
picture 22
pilot 46
places 31
plan 24
plane 67
planned 25
plants 2
play 61
playing 31
please 37
police officer 28
pony 66
popcorn 37
popular 42
Portuguese 40
postcard 22
potatoes 41
practice 10
practicing 48
prefer 37
present 20
press 73
print 22
printed 22
probably 37
promise 50
promised 50
pulled 6
put 55
puzzled 73
pyramids of Egypt 65

Q
quickly 25
quietly 25

R
raced 73
rainforest 64
ran 55
rang 4
ravioli 41
read 9
reading 3
really 16
refrigerator 19
remember 55
rented 44
restaurant 24
returned 55
rice 41
rich 42
ride 57
riding her bicycle 52
right 19
rock star 67
rocks 55
roller skating rink 60
Rome 44
room 4
run 62

S
sad 13
said 12
sale 20
Saturday 14
saw 10
say 12
says 19
scarf 2
scarves 20
school 29
second 34
secret 19
see 10
seeds 42
seeing 31
selfish 58
sell 22
send 22
sent 22
set 45
seven 50
Seven Summits 50
she'll 20
she's 2
shiny 55
shopping 24
shopping mall 37
short 38
should 20
shout 31
shouted 31
show 10
showed 22
shy 58
silly 12
simple 73
since 46
six 72
skateboard 21
ski 57
skydiving 66
sleep 24
small 60
snacks 19
snow 69
so 10
soccer 48
soccer star 72
socks 8
soda powder 6
soda water 6
sodas 19
sold 22
some 3
someday 64
someone 25
somersault 14
something 3
sometimes 59
sorry 37
sounds 37
spaghetti 9
Spain 42
Spanish 41
speak 38
speaks 38
spicy 42
spoken 40
sports 60
sports star 66
sports team 60
stand 24
starting 46
stay 14
staying 38
steak 41
stick 6
still 46
stone 55
stones 55
stood 10
stopped 34
strong 10
stronger 15
student 60
students 14
studied 47
studied Spanish 52
studies 47
studious 58
studying 52
subject 24
substitution 19
sugar 42
summer 47
Sunday 50
sure 19
surfing 67
surprise 24
surprise party 73
surprised 17

sweet 42
swim 56
swimming 52
swing 14

T
tacos 41
Taj Mahal 68
take 6
taken 46
taken a bath 53
taking 4
talk 25
talked 32
talking 3
tall 13
taught 47
teach 56
teacher 3
teaches 47
team 60
teapot 20
tell 37
ten 52
tennis 26
tennis match 17
tennis racket 26
text 37
text message 37
textbook 3
Thai 39
Thailand 39
thank 42
thank you 28
thanks 38
that 2
that's 2
the 2
theater 37
their 2
theirs 2
them 6
then 7
there 20
these 8
they 8
they're 2
things 69
think 2
third 34
this 8
those 2
thought 16
three 14
Thursday 49
ticket 37
time 6
times 7
tired 16
to 3
today 6
tomorrow 24
too 2
took 50
top 64
toys 31
traffic light 34
train station 29

trampoline 14
trapeze 14
trash 24
travel 65
treasure 31
treasure box 31
treasure hunt 31
treasure hunters 31
treasure's 31
try 17
trying 19
T-shirt 12
turn 17
turn left 30
turn right 30
turned 34
TV 9
TV show 16
TV star 66
two 30
two days 52
type 73

U
ugly 58
uncle 21
understand 73
up 14
use 19
used 42
usually 59

V
very 16
Vietnam 38
Vietnamese 38
visit 64
visiting 48

W
wait 37
waiting 37
walk 34
walked 34
walked the dog 53
walks 24
wallet 26
want 7
was 4
wash 9
washed her hands 53
wasn't 5
watch 9
water 6
watering 2
wear 26
website 31
week 48
weekend 10
welcome 14
we'll 24
well 37
went 10
were 10
we're 28
weren't 16
West 73

what 2
what's 7
when 4
where's 28
which 2
who 2
who's 17
whose 2
why 7
wild 68
will 14
window 44
winter 6
with 6
woke 17
wonderful 10
word 7
words 55
world 6
wouldn't 61
wow 46
write 19
writing 3
writing an e-mail 52
wrong 73
wrote 19

Y
year 20
years 42
yell 24
yesterday 17
yet 46
you 6
young 56
your 2
you're 20
yours 2

Z
zoo 62
zoom 73